Jessica goes to School

This edition was published by The Dreamwork Collective

The Dreamwork Collective LLC, Dubai, United Arab Emirates

thedreamworkcollective.com

Printed and bound in the United Arab Emirates by Al Ghurair Printing & Publishing

Text © Jessica Smith, 2022

Illustrations © Hasīna Shafad, 2022

Design © Alexandra Andrieș, 2022

ISBN 978-9948-764-73-1

NMC MC-02-01-6515810

Age Classification E

The content of this book is appropriate according to the age classification system issued by the Ministry of Culture and Youth.

All rights reserved. No part of this publication may be reproduced, stored, or transmitted in any form or by any means, electronic, mechanical, photo-copying, recording, or otherwise, without prior permission of the publishers.

The right of Jessica Smith to be identified as the author of this work has been asserted and protected under the UAE Copyright and Authorship Protection Law No. 7.

Dedicated to my beautiful children,
who inspire me every day to be a better version of myself.

And to everyone who has been made to feel as though
their differences were anything but a superpower . . .

Your differences are what illuminates this world.

Jessica goes to School

written by Jessica Smith
illustrated by Hasīna Shafad

THE
DREAMWORK
COLLECTIVE

Jessica woke up extra early because she was so excited. Today was her first day at school.

She pulled out her new uniform and dressed herself quicker than she had ever got dressed before.

Jessica and her three little brothers ran downstairs where mum was making breakfast.

"Are you excited about your first day at school, Jessica?" asked mum.

"Yes!
I am so excited. I can't wait to meet all my new classmates," said Jessica.

While Jessica sat and ate her breakfast, she wondered what her teacher would be like.

Once Jessica had finished eating, she grabbed her new school bag and raced to the car where her dad was waiting.
"Wait," shouted mum, "Let me help you with your shoelaces."

Jessica only had one hand and some things were hard for her to do by herself, like tying her shoelaces. But Jessica's parents were always there to help her if she needed them.

"Thanks mum, I love you," said Jessica, and off she ran.

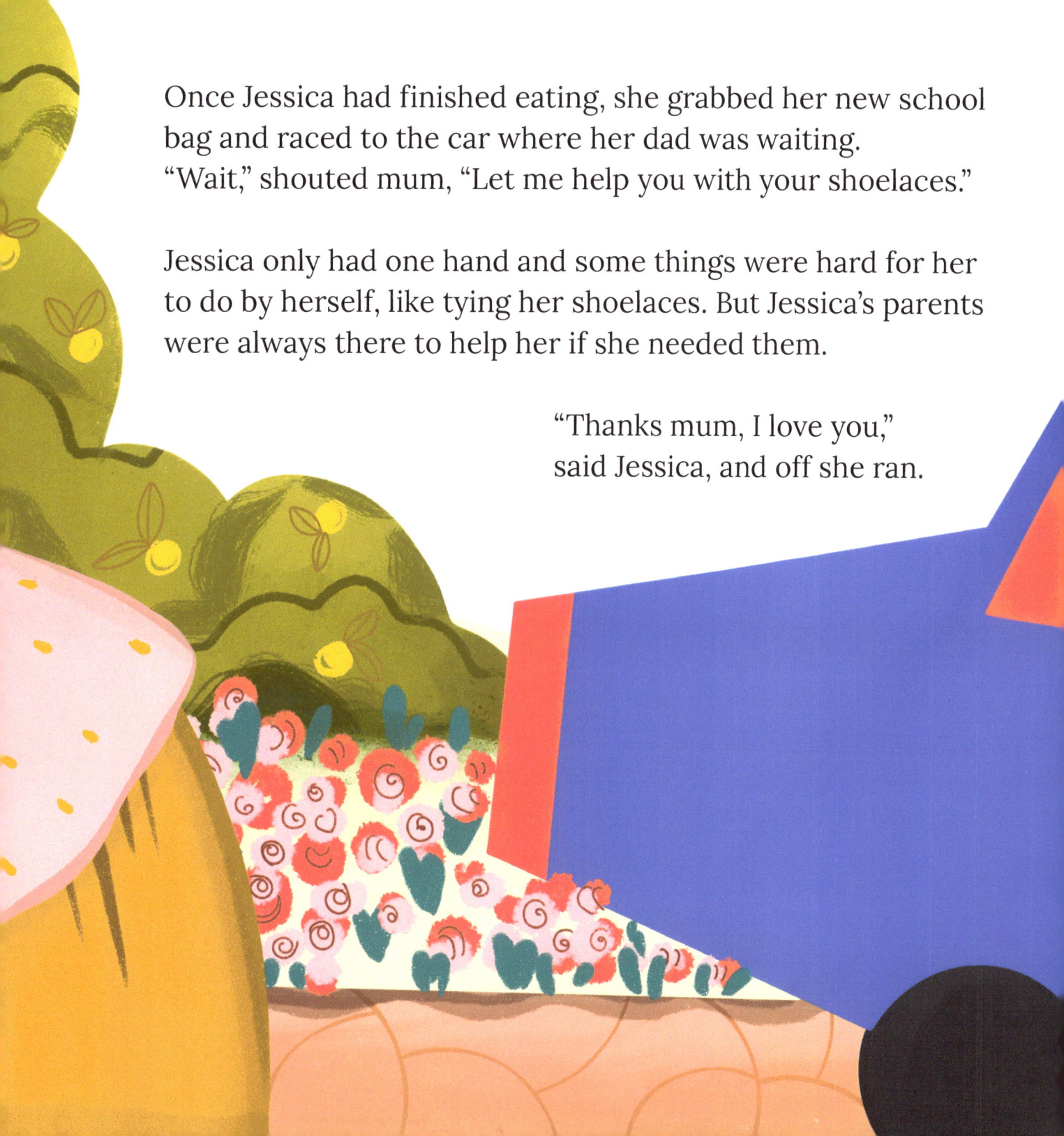

When they arrived at school, they saw lots of other girls and boys ready for their first day too.

Jessica was so excited she jumped out of the car and ran through the school gates, turning quickly to give dad a big wave.

Jessica's new teacher was Miss Fitzgerald.
She had long curly dark hair and bright blue eyes.

In class Miss Fitzgerald asked all the kids to stand up and say their name to the rest of the class.
"My name is James."
"My name is Zahra."

When it was Jessica's turn to stand up, James pointed and laughed. "That girl only has one hand," he said.

Some of the other kids started to giggle too.

Jessica was so upset she ran out of the classroom crying and sat behind a big tree so that no one could see her.

"I don't like school," she thought to herself.

Miss Fitzgerald came outside calling her name.
"Jessica, where are you?"

Jessica came out from behind the tree and told
Miss Fitzgerald that she wanted to go home.
"I don't like school," she said.
"Why not?" asked Miss Fitzgerald.
"Because the other kids laughed at me because
I only have one hand. I don't like being different,
I just want to look like everybody else."

"Sometimes people say things that they
don't mean. I'm sure James wasn't trying to
upset you on purpose," said Miss Fitzgerald.
"Let's go back inside, I want to show you something."

Miss Fitzgerald held Jessica's hand and together they walked back into the classroom. Miss Fitzgerald asked everyone in the classroom to stand up.

"Look around," she said.

"Everyone in here is different, no one looks the same as anyone else."

When Jessica looked around at the other kids, she realised that Miss Fitzgerald was right.

Everyone did look different.

Some kids had dark hair, and some had blonde hair. Some were tall and some were short.

"Sometimes I get upset too because I need to wear glasses, and they make me look different," said Zahra.

"It's good to be different," said Miss Fitzgerald, "It would be boring if we all looked the same."

"I'm different too, I wear hearing aids to help me hear," said Tara.

"I'm different too, I have lots of freckles," said Tom.

"Sometimes I don't like to play games, I prefer to read my books," said Ali.

"You see, everyone is different," said Miss Fitzgerald.

James walked over to Jessica and said,
"I didn't mean to make you cry. I've just never seen anyone with one hand before. I'm actually different too, I fell off my bike and now I have a big scar on my leg."

Jessica was so happy to see that every one of her new classmates looked different.
She wasn't upset anymore.

Later, Jessica and her new friends sat together eating their lunch.

"I think you're amazing!" said Zahra.
"I'm not amazing, I'm just Jessica."

When Jessica got home from school, she and her brothers played hide and seek together.

Mum asked, "How was your day at school?"
"My day was great! I made lots of new friends and my new teacher Miss Fitzgerald is really nice," said Jessica.

"Did you learn anything at school today?" asked Dad.

"I sure did," said Jessica.

"I learnt that it's OK to be different."

the end

Continue the conversation...

What makes you different?

Also in the *Just Jessica* series:

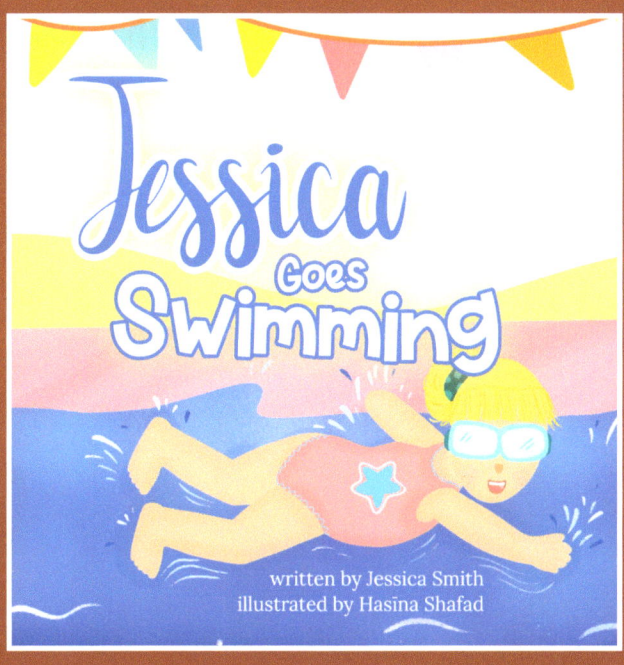

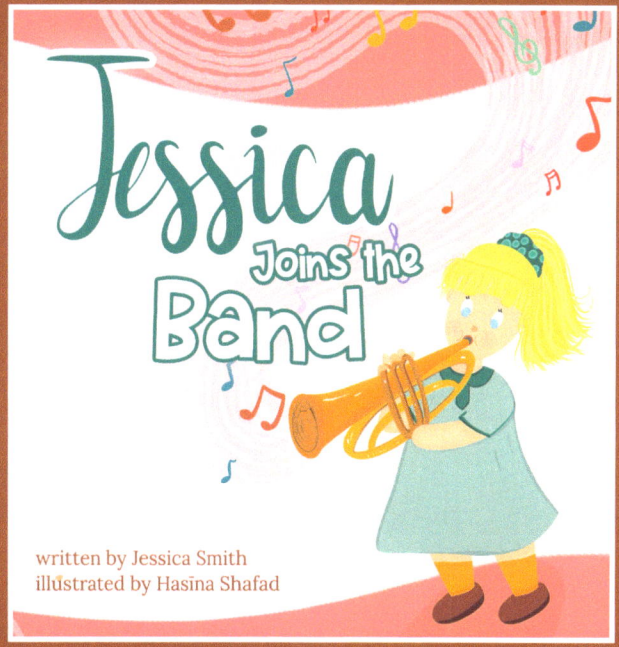

Author Bio – Jessica Smith

Jessica was born and raised in Australia, but now calls Dubai home. Born missing her left arm, Jessica focused her energy on sport and exercise as a way of proving to the world that she could overcome perceived limitations. She went on to become a Paralympic swimmer and represented Australia for 7 years. Jessica is now an internationally recognised inclusion and diversity expert. Through the Just Jessica series, the mother of 3 wants to encourage important conversations about the beauty of difference.

 **@jessicasmith27**

Illustrator Bio - Hasīna Shafad

Hasīna is an illustrator and artist based in Dubai. From cute stickers to wedding stationery and children's books, she loves to create colourful and cozy art that reflects the world around her. When she is not working, she enjoys reading, traveling, cooking and spending time with her beautiful family.

 **@turquoiseluna**

Publisher – The Dreamwork Collective

The Dreamwork Collective is a print and digital publisher sharing diverse voices and powerful stories with the world. Dedicated to the advancement of humanity, we strive to create books that have a positive impact on people and on the planet. Our hope is that our books document this moment in time for future generations to enjoy and learn from, and that we play our part in ushering humanity into a new era of heightened creativity, connection, and compassion.

 @thedreamworkcollective

www.ingramcontent.com/pod-product-compliance
Lightning Source LLC
LaVergne TN
LVHW071701060526
838201LV00038B/400